U.S. GOVERNMENT AGENCIES

WHAT DOES THE CIA DO?

DANIELLE HAYNES

PowerKiDS press

Published in 2026 by The Rosen Publishing Group, Inc.
2544 Clinton Street, Buffalo, NY 14224

First Edition

Book Design: Rachel Rising

Photo Credits: Cover, Tero Vesalainen/Shutterstock.com; Cover, pp. 1, 3–24 Madan Designer/Shutterstock.com; Cover, pp. 1, 3–24 Art Posting/Shutterstock.com; Cover, pp. 5, 7, 8, 10, 13, 15, 17, 19 Mehaniq/Shutterstock.com; p. 4 dizain/Shutterstock.com; p. 5 Only_NewPhoto/Shutterstock.com; p. 6 https://commons.wikimedia.org/wiki/File:Gilbert_Stuart_-_George_Washington_-_Google_Art_Project.jpg; p. 7 Helioscribe/Shutterstock.com; p. 9 https://commons.wikimedia.org/wiki/File:Truman_Seal_-_Flickr_-_The_Central_Intelligence_Agency.jpg; p. 9 https://commons.wikimedia.org/wiki/File:Roscoe_H._Hillenkoetter_(1957).jpg; p. 10 Rob Crandall/Shutterstock.com; p. 11 https://commons.wikimedia.org/wiki/File:John_Ratcliffe_official_photo.jpg; p. 11 John M Poltrack/Shutterstock.com; p. 12 Katherine Welles/Shutterstock.com; p. 13 https://commons.wikimedia.org/wiki/File:Aerial_view_of_CIA_headquarters,_Langley,_Virginia_14760v.jpg; p. 14 Billion Photos/Shutterstock.com; p. 15 https://commons.wikimedia.org/wiki/File:CIA_Memorial_Wall_2023.jpg; p. 16 https://en.wikipedia.org/wiki/File:Argo_poster.gif; p. 17 https://commons.wikimedia.org/wiki/File:Antonio_Joseph_Mendez_and_Jimmy_Carter.gif; p. 18 fizkes/Shutterstock.com; p. 19 Gorodenkoff/Shutterstock.com; p. 21 Inside Creative House/Shutterstock.com.

Cataloging-in-Publication Data

Names: Haynes, Danielle.
Title: What does the CIA do? / Danielle Haynes.
Description: Buffalo, New York : PowerKids Press, 2026. | Series: U.S. government agencies | Includes glossary and index.
Identifiers: ISBN 9781499453027 (pbk.) | ISBN 9781499453034 (library bound) | ISBN 9781499453041 (ebook)
Subjects: LCSH: United States. Central Intelligence Agency–Juvenile literature. | Intelligence service–United States–Juvenile literature. | Secret service–United States–Juvenile literature.
Classification: LCC JK468.I6 H38 2026 | DDC 327.1273–dc23

Manufactured in the United States of America

CPSIA Compliance Information: Batch #CSPK26. For Further Information contact Rosen Publishing at 1-800-237-9932.

CONTENTS

WHAT IS THE CIA?

Have you ever pretended to be a spy? Do you like spy movies such as *Spy Kids* or *My Spy?* But what, exactly, does a spy do? In the United States, many work for the CIA.

CIA stands for Central Intelligence Agency. It's one of 17 organizations in the U.S. government's intelligence community. You might be familiar with the word "intelligence," but it means something very particular when talking about the government. Intelligence is the information the government gathers that has military or political value. Spies often provide that intelligence to the CIA. Many types of people work for the CIA, not just spies.

AGENCY INSIGHTS

American spies who work for the U.S. government are called officers. Foreigners who provide intelligence to the CIA are called agents.

CIA officers might gather intelligence by listening to a **wiretap**.

HISTORY OF U.S. INTELLIGENCE

U.S. intelligence has existed since long before the CIA was formed. In fact, it can be traced back to the American Revolution (1765–1783). One of the first examples of **espionage** in the United States happened in 1775. General George Washington—who would go on to become the first U.S. president—paid a spy to live in Boston and report to him on the movements of British military forces.

As president, Washington asked the U.S. Congress to provide funding for an intelligence agency. Within three years, the government was spending about $1 million on intelligence.

GEORGE WASHINGTON

AGENCY INSIGHTS

Nathan Hale was executed, or killed, by the British for being a spy at age 21. His famous last words were: "I only **regret** that I have but one life to give for my country."

Nathan Hale was one of the most famous spies during the American Revolution. The British executed him for spying on them for Washington.

BIRTH OF THE CIA

For the next 150 years or so, U.S. intelligence was piecemeal. This means many different agencies collected intelligence, but no one agency oversaw everything. This approach frustrated U.S. President Franklin D. Roosevelt. So, in 1942, he created the Office of **Strategic** Services (OSS). This office oversaw all intelligence during World War II (1939–1945).

Over the next few years, the OSS was closed, and U.S. intelligence underwent many changes and had different names. Finally, President Harry S. Truman signed the National Security Act of 1947, which established the CIA. It was formed as an agency under the executive branch, independent of the military.

AGENCY INSIGHTS

The executive is one of three branches of the government. The U.S. president is the head of the executive, meaning they oversee the CIA and appoint its director.

President Truman named Roscoe H. Hillenkoetter, pictured, as the first director of the CIA.

The National Security Act of 1947 also created the job of director of central intelligence (DCI). Whoever led the CIA was also the DCI, who oversaw the entire U.S. intelligence community. They also served as an **advisor** to the president.

But in 2004, President George W. Bush changed that by creating a new role separate from director of the CIA—director of national intelligence (DNI). In 2025, President Donald Trump named Tulsi Gabbard as DNI and John Ratcliffe as director of the CIA. They both previously served in the House of Representatives in the U.S. Congress.

AGENCY INSIGHTS

During President Trump's first term in office, John Ratcliffe served as director of national intelligence.

Tulsi Gabbard (left) represented Hawaii and John Ratcliffe (right) represented Texas in Congress.

LANGLEY AND CIA STATIONS

Like many federal organizations, the CIA's headquarters is near the U.S. capital of Washington, D.C. Its main offices are in nearby Langley, Virginia. The **complex** of buildings is officially called the George Bush Center for Intelligence, but most people call it simply "Langley."

The CIA also has dozens of regional offices in foreign countries called stations. These stations usually operate out of the U.S. embassy in that country. Each of these offices has a station chief, the top CIA official in that country. Many officers and agents work for the CIA all over the world, but because the organization is so secretive, it's not clear how many.

AGENCY INSIGHTS

An embassy is the official headquarters of U.S. diplomats, or government representatives, in another country. There are more than 170 U.S. embassies all over the world.

The George Bush Center for Intelligence has two main buildings, the original headquarters at bottom left and a newer building at top right.

IT'S A SECRET

Much of what the CIA does is secretive. Officers gather lots of private information and share it with the president and other intelligence agencies both inside and outside the United States. This information helps governments make decisions on laws, foreign relations, and even war.

Some of this information can be very dangerous. For example, a foreign agent may share information with the CIA that a foreign government doesn't want anyone to know. If that foreign government found out who shared the information, that agent's life may be in danger. Some officers even live undercover, meaning they can't tell anyone they work for the CIA!

AGENCY INSIGHTS

Many Americans disagree with how secretive the CIA can be. For example, the U.S. Congress and international organizations condemned the CIA's use of secret **torture** sites in the early 2000s.

It's rare, but some CIA officers have died in the line of duty. The CIA **Memorial** Wall at Langley has a star for each of these people—140 as of 2025.

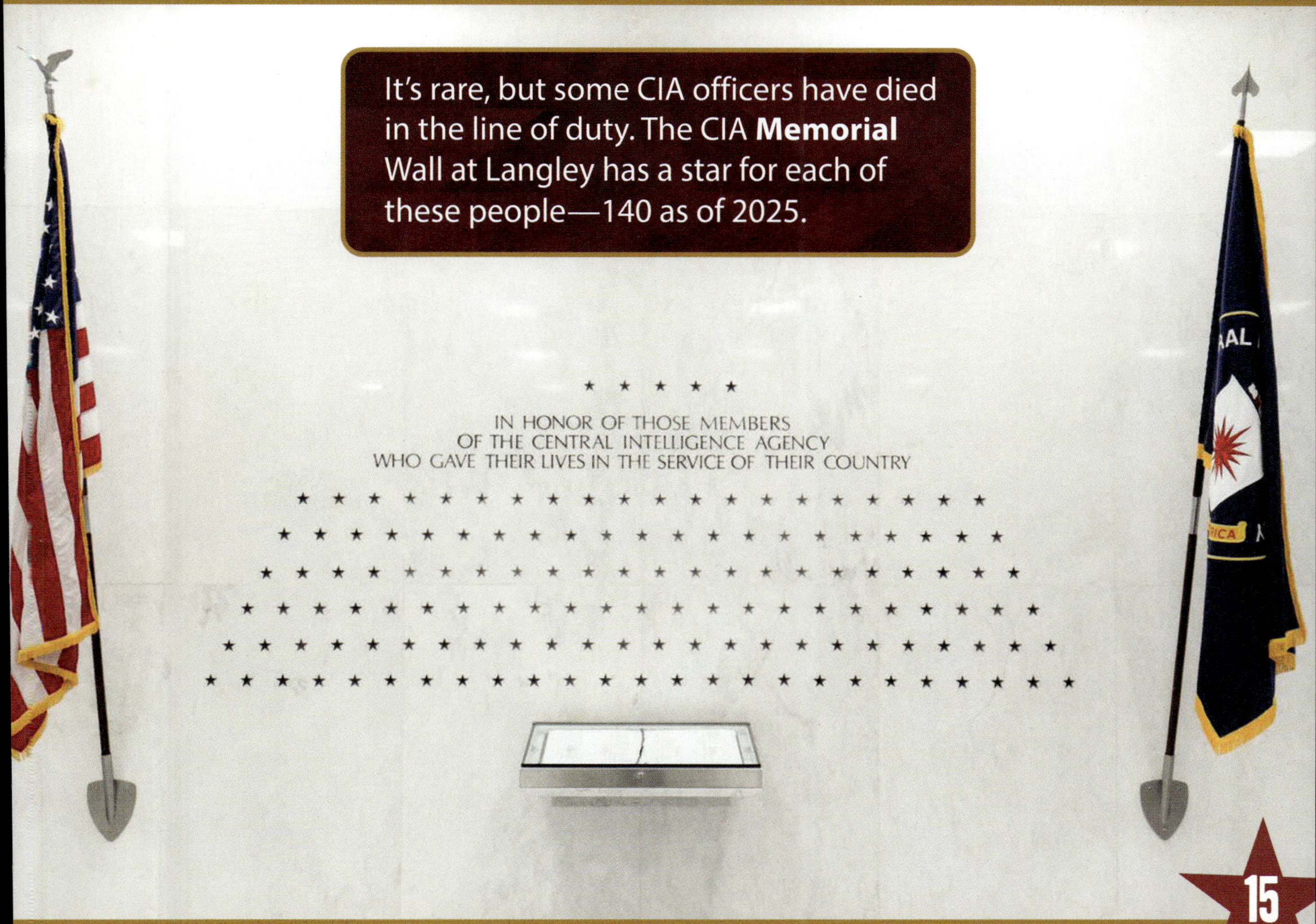

CANADIAN CAPER

One of the most famous CIA operations, the Canadian Caper, took place in Iran. In November 1979, **terrorists** took 66 Americans **hostage** at the U.S. Embassy in Tehran, Iran. Six employees of the U.S. State Department, which operated the embassy, managed to escape and hide in the homes of Canadian Embassy employees.

The CIA came up with a plan to rescue the hiding employees—called the Canadian Six—by pretending to make a movie in Tehran. CIA officers disguised themselves as a Canadian movie production team. They even set up a fake production company and named their fake movie *Argo*. The undercover CIA officers were able to save the six Americans in January 1980.

AGENCY INSIGHTS

A movie about the Canadian Caper, also called *Argo*, was made in 2012. Ben Affleck starred as CIA officer Tony Mendez.

One of the undercover CIA officers involved in the rescue mission was Tony Mendez (left). He wrote about his career in the CIA in four books.

TYPES OF JOBS

Not all people who work for the CIA do espionage work. It's a large organization with many types of employees. The CIA requires a college degree for most jobs, but that degree can be in just about any field.

Someone with a degree in the French language might be able to get a job in the CIA as a **linguist**. A person with a law degree could get a job as a lawyer within the CIA. The organization also hires medical professionals, engineers, librarians, graphic designers, and even museum workers.

There might be many types of jobs in the CIA, but they all require one thing—a background check.

AGENCY INSIGHTS

A background check involves interviewing a person's family, friends, and coworkers to determine how trustworthy a person is.

Some CIA employees operate polygraph machines. These devices are also known as lie detector machines.

A CAREER WITH THE CIA

With so many career options at the CIA, where do you start? Luckily, the agency has programs for young people to receive training. Because working for the CIA can be a very demanding and secretive job, most of these programs start once you graduate high school.

The agency offers a scholarship, or funding, to college students who commit to work for the CIA for a certain amount of time after graduation. It also has internship programs for college students.

Younger students can start exploring intelligence careers by attending summer camps that specialize in national security or government. Whatever your age, it's never too early to start reading up on the CIA and the intelligence community!

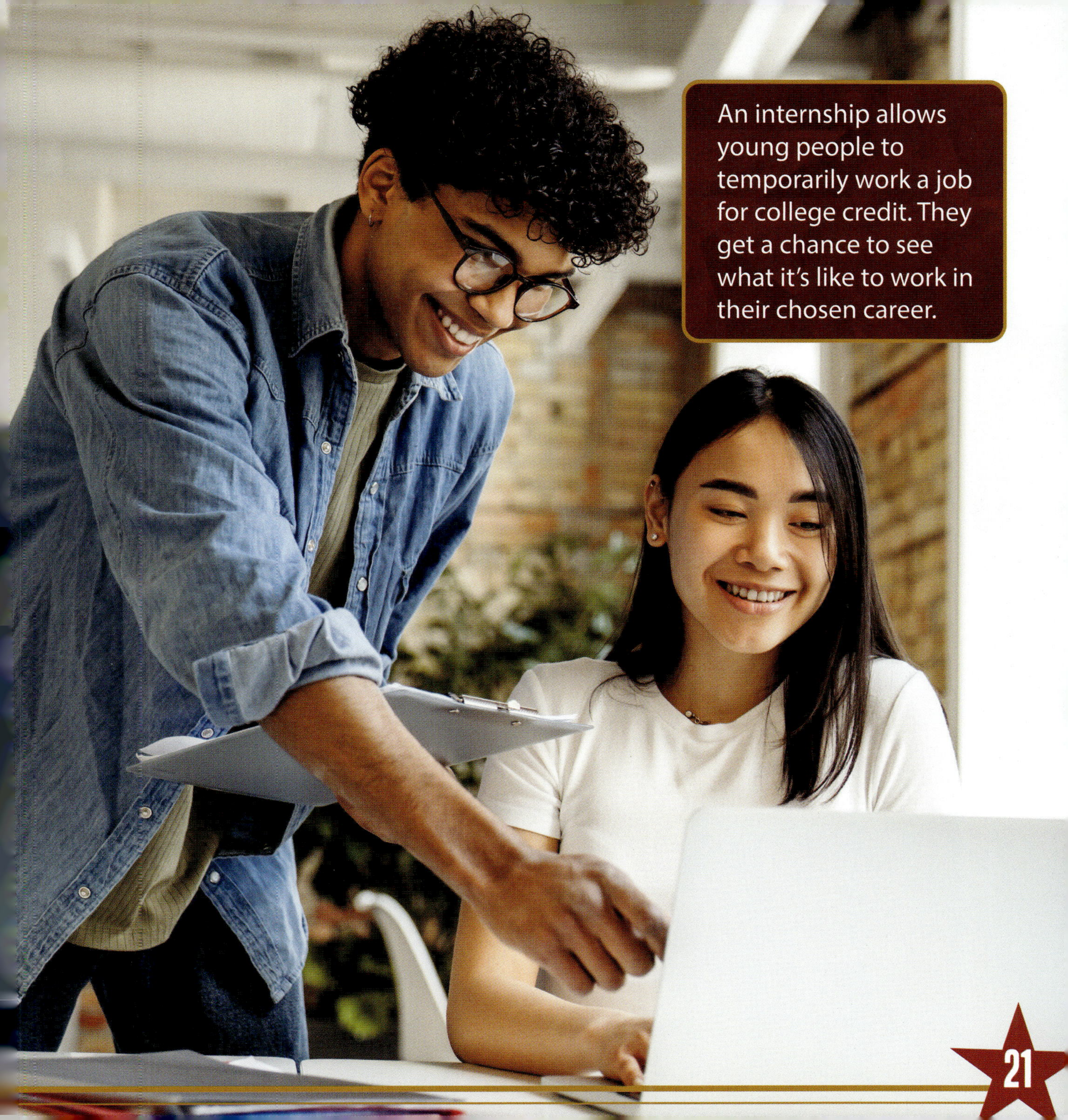

An internship allows young people to temporarily work a job for college credit. They get a chance to see what it's like to work in their chosen career.

GLOSSARY

advisor: Someone who gives advice or helps others make decisions.

complex: A building or group of buildings that have a similar purpose.

espionage: The practice of spying.

hostage: A person who is captured by someone who demands certain things before freeing the captured person.

linguist: A person who studies languages.

memorial: A monument that honors the memory of someone who has died.

regret: To be sorry.

strategic: Having a plan of action to achieve a goal.

terrorist: A person who uses violence to scare people as a way of achieving a political goal.

torture: The act of causing someone pain to get information from them.

wiretap: An electronic connection that allows a person to secretly listen to a conversation to get information.

FOR MORE INFORMATION

BOOKS

Eberth, Kristin. *The CIA*. Mankato, MN: Creative Education and Creative Paperbacks, 2025.

Gitlin, Marty. *CIA*. Mankato, MN: Bolt, 2024.

Wallmark, Laurie. *Code Breaker, Spy Hunter: How Elizabeth Friedman Changed the Course of Two World Wars*. New York, NY: Abrams Books for Young Readers, 2021.

WEBSITES

CIA: Spy Kids
www.cia.gov/spy-kids
Read more about the CIA and play games on this website.

U.S. Intelligence Community Careers
www.intelligencecareers.gov/students-and-internships
Learn more about careers and student programs in the intelligence community.

Publisher's note to educators and parents: Our editors have carefully reviewed these websites to ensure that they are suitable for students. Many websites change frequently, however, and we cannot guarantee that a site's future contents will continue to meet our high standards of quality and educational value. Be advised that students should be closely supervised whenever they access the internet.

INDEX